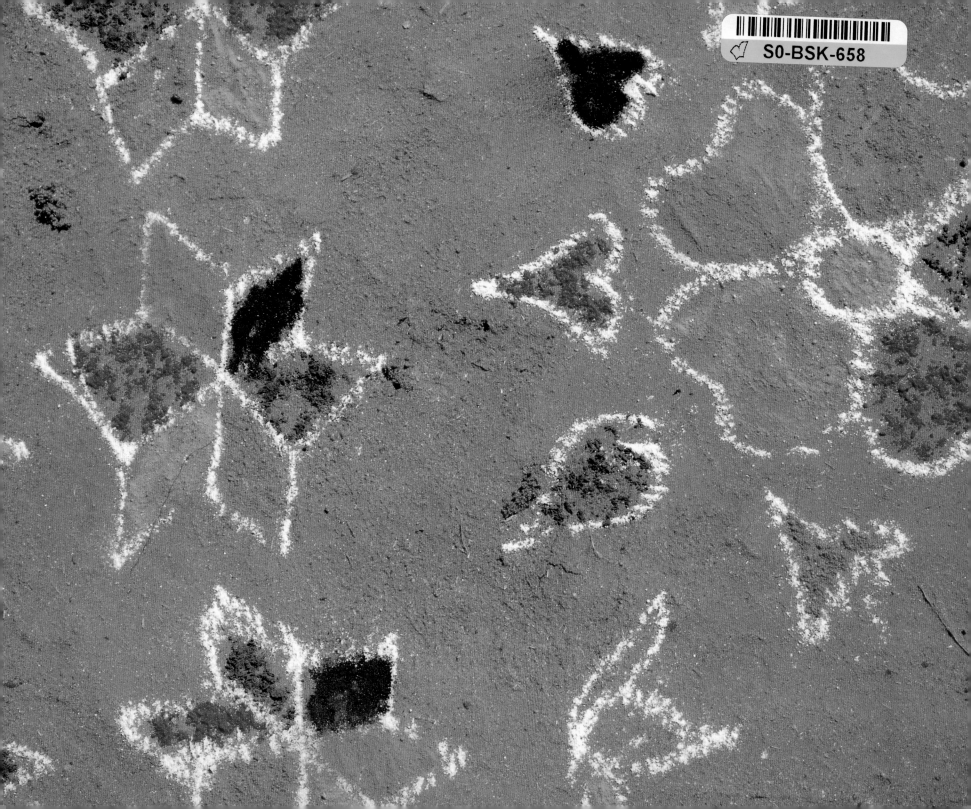

*To Amrita, Prita, Shaun and Shauna for inspiring me,
and to Yvonne for support and advice*

I is for India copyright © Frances Lincoln Limited 1996
Text and photographs copyright © Prodeepta Das 1996
The Publishers would like to acknowledge Ifeoma Onyefulu as the originator of the series
of which this book forms a part. Ifeoma Onyefulu is the author and photographer of *A is for Africa*.

First published in Great Britain in 1996 by Frances Lincoln Limited,
4 Torriano Mews, Torriano Avenue, London NW5 2RZ

British Library Cataloguing in Publication Data available on request

ISBN 0-7112-1056-X

Printed in Hong Kong

1 3 5 7 9 8 6 4 2

I is for INDIA

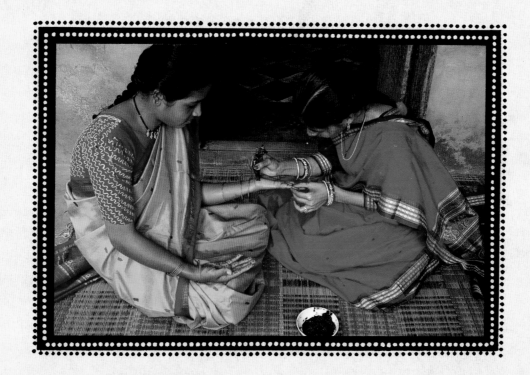

Prodeepta Das

FRANCES LINCOLN

AUTHOR'S NOTE

India is a continent with a long, rich history, now venturing bravely towards the twenty-first century.

It is full of surprising contrasts: vast open landscapes and small towns bursting at the seams; Hindus, Moslems, Sikhs, Christians and many other religions, often existing side by side, each with its own form of worship and way of life; quiet villages and sprawling cities where social changes take place at a dizzying rate. Nevertheless, some things are the same everywhere: the warmth of the people, their zest for life, and their fondness for rich colours.

I come from Orissa, in eastern India, and the words and images in this book reflect the India that I know and love. I hope they will inspire young people to go further and explore the colour, excitement and mystery of this great continent.

Prodeepta

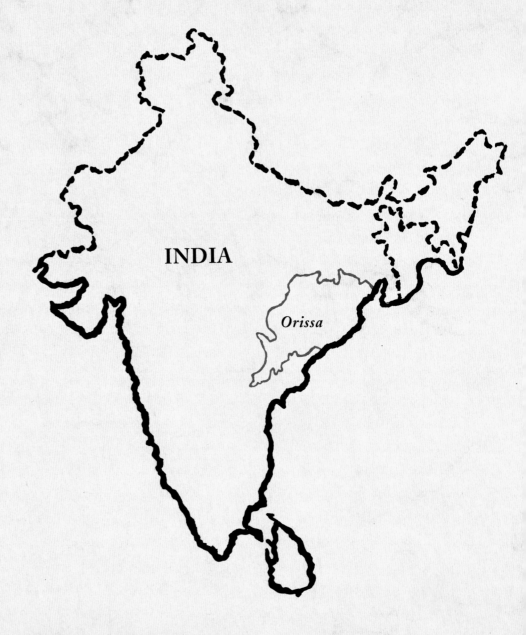

INDIA

Orissa

is for the Alphabet children learn at school. India has many languages, each with its own alphabet. These village schoolchildren are learning Oriya, the alphabet of Orissa. Their teacher writes out the first few letters on each child's slate and the children call out the letters as they go over them.

is for Bullock cart, used for carrying people and goods along the city streets and the dusty tracks of the countryside. It has two big wooden wheels and is pulled by one or two bullocks. As roads improve and people start to travel by bus, car and motorcycle, bullock carts are being used more and more for transporting goods.

is for Cinema. Most people living outside the cities have no television, so film-going is a favourite way for families to spend their spare time. Huge hoardings advertise the films showing locally and people queue for hours to see their favourite stars. Indian films are packed with song and dance.

Dd is for Diwali, the Festival of Lights - a celebration of the Hindu god Rama returning home to his kingdom after twelve years' exile. Between mid-October and mid-November, houses glow with earthen lamps, on verandahs, rooftops, walls and window-sills. Children wear new clothes for the festival and families gather to let off fireworks.

Ee

is for Elephant, an animal
feared by all other jungle creatures.
In India, the elephant has smaller
ears and teeth than the African
elephant and a hump on its forehead.
Tamed elephants have always
been used to carry people and
heavy goods. Now, as the forests
disappear and people use trucks
more and more, national parks
provide elephants with safe
places to live.

is for Family and family life, which is very strong in India. In the villages, members of several generations live under the same roof, but in crowded cities this is not always possible. Children learn early on to respect their elders, for old people have a special place in families.

G g

is for Gold, which
people love to buy and
wear. An Indian girl has
her ears pierced and wears
gold ear studs when she
is small. On marrying,
she is given gold and silver
jewellery by her relatives
and wears much of it
for her wedding.

Hh

is for Haat or markets, some held in the open air and some in covered stalls. People come from all around to buy and sell fruit, vegetables, grain, spices, clothes and many other things. Haat are cheap, colourful and extremely noisy!

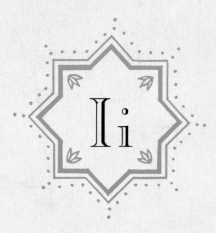

I i

is for India, a vast country
with millions of people.
They speak 17 different
languages, follow many
different religions and live
in every kind of landscape,
from hot deserts and plains
to cold mountainous areas -
but everyone is warm
and friendly and proud
to be Indian.

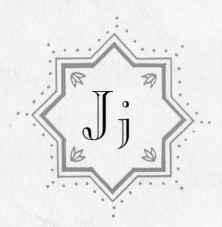

is for Jilabi, a mouth-watering, crunchy yellow sweet. To make it, the sweet-maker presses chick-pea flour batter through a mould into a deep pan of boiling oil to fry, until it looks like a fat spider's web. Then, after a dipping in sugar syrup, it is ready to eat.

is for Kameez, a loose tunic women and girls all over India like to wear. Kameez are made in many different styles and in every colour you can imagine. Some are hand-woven and decorated with beautiful embroidery.

is for Lassi, a refreshing yoghurt drink made from cow's milk.
Seasoned with salt and pepper, it is cooling and soothing,
but it tastes equally delicious sweetened with nuts and spices.

is for Mehndi, a tattoo-like decoration often worn by young women at weddings and festivals. The beautician grinds henna leaves with oil into a green paste, then squeezes the paste through a cone to make patterns on the customer's hands and feet. As the design dries, it turns bright red. It can be washed off later with water.

Nn is for Namaskar or Namaste - hands folded and held up in greeting. It is our way of saying, "I respect you."

Oo is for Odissi, an ancient traditional dance. In the past, Odissi was only performed in temples by men and women wearing special silk sarees, crowns and ankle bells. Now it can take place anywhere. It is one of the four most important Indian classical dances and takes many years of training to do well.

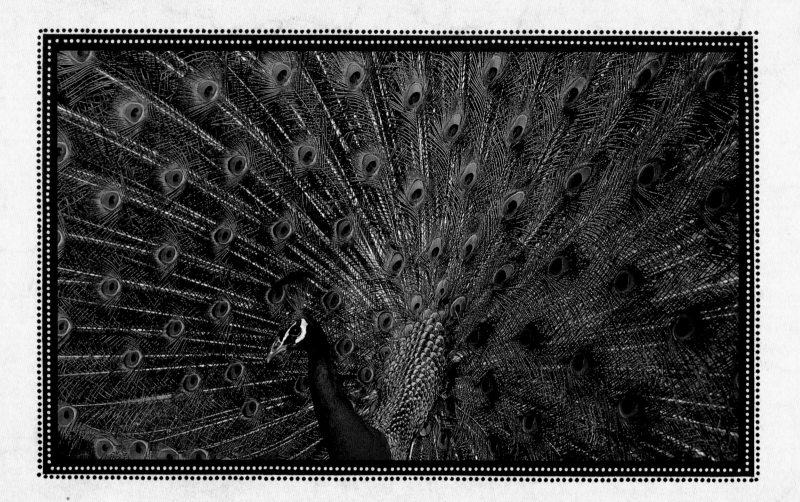

is for Peacock, India's national bird. People believe that peacocks come out to dance when it is going to rain. The birds spread out their beautiful plumes like a fan when they are courting, just before the monsoon season begins.

Qq

is for the Quran or Koran, the book
of the prophet Mohammed that
Muslim children learn when they
are very young. They sit on a prayer
mat facing in the direction of the
holy city of Mecca and read aloud
from the pages of the Quran, which
is printed in beautiful Arabic letters.

is for Rice, which we eat boiled, fried or made into cakes and puddings. We plant our rice when the rains come. Once the young green plants have turned a rich golden brown, families work together cutting, threshing and winnowing the grain. Rice is everywhere: we use it during our religious ceremonies, at weddings - we even decorate our walls and floors with coloured rice powder!

Ss

is for Sadhu or holy man. You can tell a Sadhu by his long hair and beard, the special marks on his forehead, his necklace and his loin-cloth. Sadhus have chosen to leave their families and possessions to spend all their time praying. People respect their way of life and give them food and drink. Some Sadhus stay in one place, but others travel around, sleeping in temples or outside - wherever they happen to be.

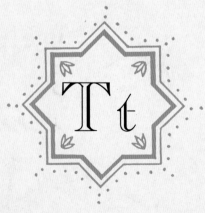

is for Tea, growing on the high slopes of eastern and southern India. Tea pickers gather only the top two leaves and a bud from the tips of each bush. Once the green leaves have been crushed and dried, they go a deep brown. On the tea stalls, tea or *chay* made with water, milk and sugar is kept brewing and served in small glasses. Some people like to add cardamom and ginger to make masala tea.

U u is for Umbrella, used not only when it rains but also to give shade from the hot sun. The most beautiful umbrellas are made in a small village in Orissa called Pipili.

V v is for Veena, an ancient Indian musical instrument with seven strings. It is made from a piece of jackfruit wood, with a hollow at the top end. The veena takes many years to learn to play.

is for Water. In the rainy
season there is too much of it,
and in the dry season too little.
Many towns only receive piped
water for a few hours each
day, so everyone stores it in
big containers to last the rest
of the day. In the villages,
people collect rain water
in tanks or sink deep wells.
We use our rivers, canals and
ponds for washing, growing
crops and keeping our cattle
clean, and we do our ritual
bathing in the holy river at
Varanasi and in the sea at Puri.

is for Xmas, as Christmas is usually known in India. It is a time when Christian families gather together to receive presents from Father Xmas and to pose solemnly for the great family photograph. In southern India, Xmas is celebrated in January.

is for Yatra, a religious fair often held in a temple. Pilgrims, holy men and people of all ages come from near and far to worship, listen to songs of prayer and watch shows based on stories from holy books. Sometimes, when a yatra goes on for a few days, people sleep outside in tents.

Z is for the Zodiac of twelve birth signs. When a baby is born,
the parents call in an astrologer. The astrologer makes calculations
in chalk on the floor, writing down on a palm leaf with an iron pen
the baby's sign and what will happen when he or she grows up.
The leaf is then wrapped in a clean cloth and the parents treasure
it together with their own hopes for the baby's future.

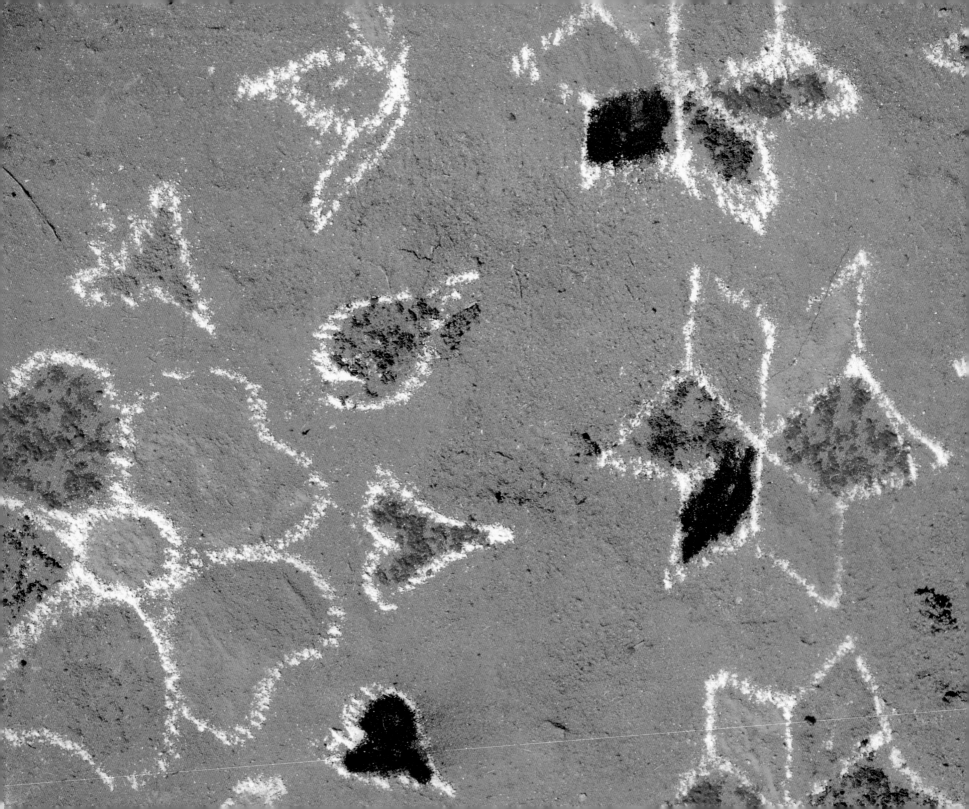